Welcome

Please sign our guest book and share your experience with us.

Welcome

Guest Name(s):_____ Date(s) of your stay:_____

Traveled From: _____

Favorite Beach House Memories:_____

_____

_____

_____

_____

_____

_____

_____

Recommendations (restaurants, entertainment, must-see sites):_____

_____

_____

_____

_____

_____

_____

_____

Message to the Host:_____

_____

_____

_____

_____

_____

Welcome

Guest Name(s):_____ Date(s) of your stay:_____

Traveled From: _____

Favorite Beach House Memories: _____

_____

_____

_____

_____

_____

_____

Recommendations (restaurants, entertainment, must-see sites): _____

_____

_____

_____

_____

_____

_____

Message to the Host:_____

_____

_____

_____

_____

Welcome

Guest Name(s):_____ Date(s) of your stay:_____

Traveled From: _____

Favorite Beach House Memories:_____

_____

_____

_____

_____

_____

_____

Recommendations (restaurants, entertainment, must-see sites):_____

_____

_____

_____

_____

_____

_____

Message to the Host:_____

_____

_____

_____

_____

_____

Welcome

Guest Name(s):_____ Date(s) of your stay:_____

Traveled From: _____

Favorite Beach House Memories:_____

_____

_____

_____

_____

_____

_____

_____

Recommendations (restaurants, entertainment, must-see sites):_____

_____

_____

_____

_____

_____

_____

_____

Message to the Host:_____

_____

_____

_____

_____

Welcome

Guest Name(s):_____ Date(s) of your stay:_____

Traveled From: _____

Favorite Beach House Memories:_____

_____

_____

_____

_____

_____

_____

_____

Recommendations (restaurants, entertainment, must-see sites):_____

_____

_____

_____

_____

_____

_____

_____

Message to the Host:_____

_____

_____

_____

_____

_____

_____

Welcome

Guest Name(s):_____ Date(s) of your stay:_____

Traveled From: _____

Favorite Beach House Memories: _____
_____
_____
_____
_____
_____
_____

Recommendations (restaurants, entertainment, must-see sites): _____
_____
_____
_____
_____
_____
_____

Message to the Host:_____
_____
_____
_____
_____

Welcome

Guest Name(s):_____ Date(s) of your stay:_____

Traveled From: _____

Favorite Beach House Memories:_____

_____
_____
_____
_____
_____
_____

Recommendations (restaurants, entertainment, must-see sites):_____

_____
_____
_____
_____
_____
_____

Message to the Host:_____

_____
_____
_____
_____
_____

Welcome

Guest Name(s):_____ Date(s) of your stay:_____

Traveled From: _____

Favorite Beach House Memories: _____
_____
_____
_____
_____
_____
_____
_____

Recommendations (restaurants, entertainment, must-see sites): _____
_____
_____
_____
_____
_____
_____
_____

Message to the Host: _____
_____
_____
_____
_____
_____

Welcome

Guest Name(s):_____ Date(s) of your stay:_____

Traveled From: _____

Favorite Beach House Memories: _____

_____

_____

_____

_____

_____

_____

_____

Recommendations (restaurants, entertainment, must-see sites): _____

_____

_____

_____

_____

_____

_____

_____

Message to the Host:_____

_____

_____

_____

_____

_____

Welcome

Guest Name(s):_____ Date(s) of your stay:_____

Traveled From: _____

Favorite Beach House Memories:_____
_____
_____
_____
_____
_____
_____

Recommendations (restaurants, entertainment, must-see sites):_____
_____
_____
_____
_____
_____
_____
_____

Message to the Host:_____
_____
_____
_____
_____

Welcome

Guest Name(s):_____ Date(s) of your stay:_____

Traveled From: _____

Favorite Beach House Memories: _____

_____

_____

_____

_____

_____

_____

_____

Recommendations (restaurants, entertainment, must-see sites): _____

_____

_____

_____

_____

_____

_____

_____

Message to the Host:_____

_____

_____

_____

_____

_____

Welcome

Guest Name(s):_____ Date(s) of your stay:_____

Traveled From: _____

Favorite Beach House Memories: _____

_____

_____

_____

_____

_____

_____

_____

Recommendations (restaurants, entertainment, must-see sites): _____

_____

_____

_____

_____

_____

_____

_____

Message to the Host:_____

_____

_____

_____

_____

_____

Welcome

Guest Name(s):_____ Date(s) of your stay:_____

Traveled From: _____

Favorite Beach House Memories:_____

_____

_____

_____

_____

_____

_____

_____

Recommendations (restaurants, entertainment, must-see sites):_____

_____

_____

_____

_____

_____

_____

_____

_____

Message to the Host:_____

_____

_____

_____

_____

_____

Welcome

Guest Name(s):_____ Date(s) of your stay:_____

Traveled From: _____

Favorite Beach House Memories:_____

_____

_____

_____

_____

_____

_____

Recommendations (restaurants, entertainment, must-see sites):_____

_____

_____

_____

_____

_____

_____

Message to the Host:_____

_____

_____

_____

_____

Welcome

Guest Name(s):_____ Date(s) of your stay:_____

Traveled From: _____

Favorite Beach House Memories:_____

_____

_____

_____

_____

_____

_____

Recommendations (restaurants, entertainment, must-see sites):_____

_____

_____

_____

_____

_____

_____

Message to the Host:_____

_____

_____

_____

_____

_____

Welcome

Guest Name(s):_____ Date(s) of your stay:_____

Traveled From: _____

Favorite Beach House Memories:_____
_____
_____
_____
_____
_____
_____
_____

Recommendations (restaurants, entertainment, must-see sites):_____
_____
_____
_____
_____
_____
_____
_____

Message to the Host:_____
_____
_____
_____
_____
_____

Welcome

Guest Name(s):_____ Date(s) of your stay:_____

Traveled From: _____

Favorite Beach House Memories:_____

_____

_____

_____

_____

_____

_____

_____

Recommendations (restaurants, entertainment, must-see sites):_____

_____

_____

_____

_____

_____

_____

_____

Message to the Host:_____

_____

_____

_____

_____

_____

Welcome

Guest Name(s):_____ Date(s) of your stay:_____

Traveled From: _____

Favorite Beach House Memories: _____
_____
_____
_____
_____
_____
_____
_____

Recommendations (restaurants, entertainment, must-see sites): _____
_____
_____
_____
_____
_____
_____
_____

Message to the Host:_____
_____
_____
_____
_____
_____

Welcome

Guest Name(s):_____ Date(s) of your stay:_____

Traveled From: _____

Favorite Beach House Memories:_____

_____

_____

_____

_____

_____

_____

_____

Recommendations (restaurants, entertainment, must-see sites):_____

_____

_____

_____

_____

_____

_____

_____

Message to the Host:_____

_____

_____

_____

_____

_____

Welcome

Guest Name(s):_____ Date(s) of your stay:_____

Traveled From: _____

Favorite Beach House Memories: _____

_____

_____

_____

_____

_____

_____

Recommendations (restaurants, entertainment, must-see sites):_____

_____

_____

_____

_____

_____

_____

Message to the Host:_____

_____

_____

_____

_____

Welcome

Guest Name(s):_____ Date(s) of your stay:_____

Traveled From: _____

Favorite Beach House Memories:_____
_____
_____
_____
_____
_____
_____
_____

Recommendations (restaurants, entertainment, must-see sites):_____
_____
_____
_____
_____
_____
_____
_____

Message to the Host:_____
_____
_____
_____
_____
_____

Welcome

Guest Name(s):_____ Date(s) of your stay:_____

Traveled From: _____

Favorite Beach House Memories:_____
_____
_____
_____
_____
_____
_____
_____

Recommendations (restaurants, entertainment, must-see sites):_____
_____
_____
_____
_____
_____
_____
_____

Message to the Host:_____
_____
_____
_____
_____
_____

Welcome

Guest Name(s):_____ Date(s) of your stay:_____

Traveled From: _____

Favorite Beach House Memories: _____

_____
_____
_____
_____
_____
_____
_____

Recommendations (restaurants, entertainment, must-see sites): _____

_____
_____
_____
_____
_____
_____
_____

Message to the Host:_____

_____
_____
_____
_____
_____

Welcome

Guest Name(s):_____ Date(s) of your stay:_____

Traveled From: _____

Favorite Beach House Memories: _____

_____
_____
_____
_____
_____
_____
_____

Recommendations (restaurants, entertainment, must-see sites):_____

_____
_____
_____
_____
_____
_____
_____

Message to the Host:_____

_____
_____
_____
_____

Welcome

Guest Name(s):_____ Date(s) of your stay:_____

Traveled From: _____

Favorite Beach House Memories:_____

_____

_____

_____

_____

_____

_____

Recommendations (restaurants, entertainment, must-see sites):_____

_____

_____

_____

_____

_____

_____

_____

Message to the Host:_____

_____

_____

_____

_____

_____

Welcome

Guest Name(s):_____ Date(s) of your stay:_____

Traveled From: _____

Favorite Beach House Memories: _____

_____

_____

_____

_____

_____

_____

_____

Recommendations (restaurants, entertainment, must-see sites): _____

_____

_____

_____

_____

_____

_____

_____

Message to the Host:_____

_____

_____

_____

_____

_____

Welcome

Guest Name(s):_____ Date(s) of your stay:_____

Traveled From: _____

Favorite Beach House Memories:_____

_____

_____

_____

_____

_____

_____

Recommendations (restaurants, entertainment, must-see sites):_____

_____

_____

_____

_____

_____

_____

Message to the Host:_____

_____

_____

_____

_____

Welcome

Guest Name(s):_____ Date(s) of your stay:_____

Traveled From: _____

Favorite Beach House Memories: _____
_____
_____
_____
_____
_____
_____
_____

Recommendations (restaurants, entertainment, must-see sites): _____
_____
_____
_____
_____
_____
_____
_____

Message to the Host:_____
_____
_____
_____
_____
_____

Welcome

Guest Name(s):_____ Date(s) of your stay:_____

Traveled From: _____

Favorite Beach House Memories: _____

_____

_____

_____

_____

_____

_____

Recommendations (restaurants, entertainment, must-see sites): _____

_____

_____

_____

_____

_____

Message to the Host:_____

_____

_____

_____

_____

Welcome

Guest Name(s):_____ Date(s) of your stay:_____

Traveled From: _____

Favorite Beach House Memories:_____

_____
_____
_____
_____
_____
_____
_____

Recommendations (restaurants, entertainment, must-see sites):_____

_____
_____
_____
_____
_____
_____
_____

Message to the Host:_____

_____
_____
_____
_____
_____

Welcome

Guest Name(s):_____ Date(s) of your stay:_____

Traveled From: _____

Favorite Beach House Memories: _____

_____
_____
_____
_____
_____
_____
_____

Recommendations (restaurants, entertainment, must-see sites): _____

_____
_____
_____
_____
_____
_____
_____

Message to the Host:_____

_____
_____
_____
_____
_____

Welcome

Guest Name(s):_____ Date(s) of your stay:_____

Traveled From: _____

Favorite Beach House Memories:_____

_____
_____
_____
_____
_____
_____
_____

Recommendations (restaurants, entertainment, must-see sites):_____

_____
_____
_____
_____
_____
_____
_____

Message to the Host:_____

_____
_____
_____
_____

Welcome

Guest Name(s):_____ Date(s) of your stay:_____

Traveled From: _____

Favorite Beach House Memories:_____

_____
_____
_____
_____
_____
_____
_____

Recommendations (restaurants, entertainment, must-see sites):_____

_____
_____
_____
_____
_____
_____
_____

Message to the Host:_____

_____
_____
_____
_____
_____
_____

Welcome

Guest Name(s):_____ Date(s) of your stay:_____

Traveled From: _____

Favorite Beach House Memories: _____
_____
_____
_____
_____
_____
_____
_____
_____

Recommendations (restaurants, entertainment, must-see sites):_____
_____
_____
_____
_____
_____
_____
_____
_____

Message to the Host:_____
_____
_____
_____
_____
_____

Welcome

Guest Name(s):_____ Date(s) of your stay:_____

Traveled From: _____

Favorite Beach House Memories:_____

_____

_____

_____

_____

_____

_____

_____

Recommendations (restaurants, entertainment, must-see sites):_____

_____

_____

_____

_____

_____

_____

_____

Message to the Host:_____

_____

_____

_____

_____

_____

Welcome

Guest Name(s):_____ Date(s) of your stay:_____

Traveled From: _____

Favorite Beach House Memories:_____

_____
_____
_____
_____
_____
_____
_____

Recommendations (restaurants, entertainment, must-see sites):_____

_____
_____
_____
_____
_____
_____
_____

Message to the Host:_____

_____
_____
_____
_____
_____

Welcome

Guest Name(s):_____ Date(s) of your stay:_____

Traveled From: _____

Favorite Beach House Memories:_____

_____

_____

_____

_____

_____

_____

_____

Recommendations (restaurants, entertainment, must-see sites):_____

_____

_____

_____

_____

_____

_____

_____

Message to the Host:_____

_____

_____

_____

_____

Welcome

Guest Name(s):_____ Date(s) of your stay:_____

Traveled From: _____

Favorite Beach House Memories:_____

_____
_____
_____
_____
_____
_____

Recommendations (restaurants, entertainment, must-see sites):_____

_____
_____
_____
_____
_____
_____

Message to the Host:_____

_____
_____
_____
_____

Welcome

Guest Name(s):_____ Date(s) of your stay:_____

Traveled From: _____

Favorite Beach House Memories: _____

_____
_____
_____
_____
_____
_____
_____

Recommendations (restaurants, entertainment, must-see sites): _____

_____
_____
_____
_____
_____
_____
_____
_____

Message to the Host:_____

_____
_____
_____
_____
_____

Welcome

Guest Name(s):_____ Date(s) of your stay:_____

Traveled From: _____

Favorite Beach House Memories:_____
_____
_____
_____
_____
_____
_____
_____

Recommendations (restaurants, entertainment, must-see sites):_____
_____
_____
_____
_____
_____
_____
_____

Message to the Host:_____
_____
_____
_____
_____
_____

Welcome

Guest Name(s):_____ Date(s) of your stay:_____

Traveled From: _____

Favorite Beach House Memories: _____

_____

_____

_____

_____

_____

_____

Recommendations (restaurants, entertainment, must-see sites): _____

_____

_____

_____

_____

_____

_____

Message to the Host:_____

_____

_____

_____

_____

_____

Welcome

Guest Name(s):_____ Date(s) of your stay:_____

Traveled From: _____

Favorite Beach House Memories:_____

_____
_____
_____
_____
_____
_____
_____

Recommendations (restaurants, entertainment, must-see sites):_____

_____
_____
_____
_____
_____
_____
_____

Message to the Host:_____

_____
_____
_____
_____
_____

Welcome

Guest Name(s):_____ Date(s) of your stay:_____

Traveled From: _____

Favorite Beach House Memories:_____

_____

_____

_____

_____

_____

_____

_____

Recommendations (restaurants, entertainment, must-see sites):_____

_____

_____

_____

_____

_____

_____

_____

Message to the Host:_____

_____

_____

_____

_____

_____

Welcome

Guest Name(s):_____ Date(s) of your stay:_____

Traveled From: _____

Favorite Beach House Memories:_____

_____

_____

_____

_____

_____

_____

_____

Recommendations (restaurants, entertainment, must-see sites):_____

_____

_____

_____

_____

_____

_____

_____

Message to the Host:_____

_____

_____

_____

_____

_____

Welcome

Guest Name(s):_____ Date(s) of your stay:_____

Traveled From: _____

Favorite Beach House Memories:_____

_____

_____

_____

_____

_____

_____

_____

Recommendations (restaurants, entertainment, must-see sites):_____

_____

_____

_____

_____

_____

_____

_____

_____

Message to the Host:_____

_____

_____

_____

_____

_____

Welcome

Guest Name(s):_____ Date(s) of your stay:_____

Traveled From: _____

Favorite Beach House Memories:_____

_____
_____
_____
_____
_____
_____
_____

Recommendations (restaurants, entertainment, must-see sites):_____

_____
_____
_____
_____
_____
_____
_____

Message to the Host:_____

_____
_____
_____
_____

Welcome

Guest Name(s):_____ Date(s) of your stay:_____

Traveled From: _____

Favorite Beach House Memories:_____

_____

_____

_____

_____

_____

_____

Recommendations (restaurants, entertainment, must-see sites):_____

_____

_____

_____

_____

_____

_____

Message to the Host:_____

_____

_____

_____

_____

Welcome

Guest Name(s):_____ Date(s) of your stay:_____

Traveled From: _____

Favorite Beach House Memories: _____

_____

_____

_____

_____

_____

_____

Recommendations (restaurants, entertainment, must-see sites): _____

_____

_____

_____

_____

_____

_____

_____

Message to the Host: _____

_____

_____

_____

_____

_____

Welcome

Guest Name(s):_____ Date(s) of your stay:_____

Traveled From: _____

Favorite Beach House Memories: _____

_____

_____

_____

_____

_____

_____

_____

Recommendations (restaurants, entertainment, must-see sites): _____

_____

_____

_____

_____

_____

_____

_____

Message to the Host:_____

_____

_____

_____

_____

_____

Welcome

Guest Name(s):_____ Date(s) of your stay:_____

Traveled From: _____

Favorite Beach House Memories:_____
_____
_____
_____
_____
_____
_____
_____

Recommendations (restaurants, entertainment, must-see sites):_____
_____
_____
_____
_____
_____
_____
_____

Message to the Host:_____
_____
_____
_____
_____

Welcome

Guest Name(s):_____ Date(s) of your stay:_____

Traveled From: _____

Favorite Beach House Memories:_____

_____

_____

_____

_____

_____

_____

_____

Recommendations (restaurants, entertainment, must-see sites):_____

_____

_____

_____

_____

_____

_____

_____

Message to the Host:_____

_____

_____

_____

_____

_____

Welcome

Guest Name(s):_____ Date(s) of your stay:_____

Traveled From: _____

Favorite Beach House Memories:_____

_____

_____

_____

_____

_____

_____

_____

Recommendations (restaurants, entertainment, must-see sites): _____

_____

_____

_____

_____

_____

_____

_____

Message to the Host:_____

_____

_____

_____

_____

_____

Welcome

Guest Name(s):_____ Date(s) of your stay:_____

Traveled From: _____

Favorite Beach House Memories:_____

_____

_____

_____

_____

_____

_____

_____

Recommendations (restaurants, entertainment, must-see sites):_____

_____

_____

_____

_____

_____

_____

_____

_____

Message to the Host:_____

_____

_____

_____

_____

_____

Welcome

Guest Name(s):_____ Date(s) of your stay:_____

Traveled From: _____

Favorite Beach House Memories:_____

_____

_____

_____

_____

_____

_____

_____

Recommendations (restaurants, entertainment, must-see sites):_____

_____

_____

_____

_____

_____

_____

Message to the Host:_____

_____

_____

_____

_____

_____

Welcome

Guest Name(s):_____ Date(s) of your stay:_____

Traveled From: _____

Favorite Beach House Memories:_____

_____
_____
_____
_____
_____
_____
_____

Recommendations (restaurants, entertainment, must-see sites):_____

_____
_____
_____
_____
_____
_____
_____

Message to the Host:_____

_____
_____
_____
_____

Welcome

Guest Name(s):_____ Date(s) of your stay:_____

Traveled From: _____

Favorite Beach House Memories: _____

_____

_____

_____

_____

_____

_____

Recommendations (restaurants, entertainment, must-see sites):_____

_____

_____

_____

_____

_____

_____

Message to the Host:_____

_____

_____

_____

_____

Welcome

Guest Name(s):_____ Date(s) of your stay:_____

Traveled From: _____

Favorite Beach House Memories: _____

_____
_____
_____
_____
_____
_____
_____

Recommendations (restaurants, entertainment, must-see sites): _____

_____
_____
_____
_____
_____
_____
_____

Message to the Host:_____

_____
_____
_____
_____
_____

Welcome

Guest Name(s):_____ Date(s) of your stay:_____

Traveled From: _____

Favorite Beach House Memories:_____

_____
_____
_____
_____
_____
_____
_____

Recommendations (restaurants, entertainment, must-see sites):_____

_____
_____
_____
_____
_____
_____
_____

Message to the Host:_____

_____
_____
_____
_____
_____

Welcome

Guest Name(s):_____ Date(s) of your stay:_____

Traveled From: _____

Favorite Beach House Memories: _____
_____
_____
_____
_____
_____
_____

Recommendations (restaurants, entertainment, must-see sites): _____
_____
_____
_____
_____
_____
_____
_____

Message to the Host: _____
_____
_____
_____
_____
_____

Welcome

Guest Name(s):_____ Date(s) of your stay:_____

Traveled From: _____

Favorite Beach House Memories:_____

_____
_____
_____
_____
_____
_____
_____

Recommendations (restaurants, entertainment, must-see sites):_____

_____
_____
_____
_____
_____
_____
_____

Message to the Host:_____

_____
_____
_____
_____
_____

Welcome

Guest Name(s):_____ Date(s) of your stay:_____

Traveled From: _____

Favorite Beach House Memories:_____

_____

_____

_____

_____

_____

_____

Recommendations (restaurants, entertainment, must-see sites):_____

_____

_____

_____

_____

_____

_____

Message to the Host:_____

_____

_____

_____

_____

_____

Welcome

Guest Name(s):_____ Date(s) of your stay:_____

Traveled From: _____

Favorite Beach House Memories:_____

_____

_____

_____

_____

_____

_____

_____

Recommendations (restaurants, entertainment, must-see sites):_____

_____

_____

_____

_____

_____

_____

_____

Message to the Host:_____

_____

_____

_____

_____

Welcome

Guest Name(s):_____ Date(s) of your stay:_____

Traveled From: _____

Favorite Beach House Memories: _____

_____

_____

_____

_____

_____

_____

Recommendations (restaurants, entertainment, must-see sites): _____

_____

_____

_____

_____

_____

_____

Message to the Host:_____

_____

_____

_____

_____

_____

Welcome

Guest Name(s):_____ Date(s) of your stay:_____

Traveled From: _____

Favorite Beach House Memories:_____
_____
_____
_____
_____
_____
_____
_____

Recommendations (restaurants, entertainment, must-see sites):_____
_____
_____
_____
_____
_____
_____
_____

Message to the Host:_____
_____
_____
_____
_____
_____

Welcome

Guest Name(s):_____ Date(s) of your stay:_____

Traveled From: _____

Favorite Beach House Memories: _____
_____
_____
_____
_____
_____
_____

Recommendations (restaurants, entertainment, must-see sites): _____
_____
_____
_____
_____
_____
_____

Message to the Host: _____
_____
_____
_____
_____

Welcome

Guest Name(s):_____ Date(s) of your stay:_____

Traveled From: _____

Favorite Beach House Memories:_____

_____

_____

_____

_____

_____

_____

_____

Recommendations (restaurants, entertainment, must-see sites):_____

_____

_____

_____

_____

_____

_____

_____

Message to the Host:_____

_____

_____

_____

_____

Welcome

Guest Name(s):_____ Date(s) of your stay:_____

Traveled From: _____

Favorite Beach House Memories:_____

_____

_____

_____

_____

_____

_____

_____

Recommendations (restaurants, entertainment, must-see sites):_____

_____

_____

_____

_____

_____

_____

_____

Message to the Host:_____

_____

_____

_____

_____

_____

Welcome

Guest Name(s):_____ Date(s) of your stay:_____

Traveled From: _____

Favorite Beach House Memories:_____

_____

_____

_____

_____

_____

_____

Recommendations (restaurants, entertainment, must-see sites):_____

_____

_____

_____

_____

_____

_____

Message to the Host:_____

_____

_____

_____

_____

Welcome

Guest Name(s):_____ Date(s) of your stay:_____

Traveled From: _____

Favorite Beach House Memories:_____

_____
_____
_____
_____
_____
_____
_____

Recommendations (restaurants, entertainment, must-see sites):_____

_____
_____
_____
_____
_____
_____
_____

Message to the Host:_____

_____
_____
_____
_____
_____

Welcome

Guest Name(s):_____ Date(s) of your stay:_____

Traveled From: _____

Favorite Beach House Memories: _____
_____
_____
_____
_____
_____
_____
_____

Recommendations (restaurants, entertainment, must-see sites): _____
_____
_____
_____
_____
_____
_____
_____

Message to the Host:_____
_____
_____
_____
_____
_____

Welcome

Guest Name(s):_____ Date(s) of your stay:_____

Traveled From: _____

Favorite Beach House Memories:_____

_____

_____

_____

_____

_____

_____

_____

Recommendations (restaurants, entertainment, must-see sites):_____

_____

_____

_____

_____

_____

_____

Message to the Host:_____

_____

_____

_____

_____

Welcome

Guest Name(s):_____ Date(s) of your stay:_____

Traveled From: _____

Favorite Beach House Memories: _____
_____
_____
_____
_____
_____
_____
_____

Recommendations (restaurants, entertainment, must-see sites): _____
_____
_____
_____
_____
_____
_____

Message to the Host:_____
_____
_____
_____
_____

Welcome

Guest Name(s):_____ Date(s) of your stay:_____

Traveled From: _____

Favorite Beach House Memories:_____
_____
_____
_____
_____
_____
_____
_____
_____

Recommendations (restaurants, entertainment, must-see sites): _____
_____
_____
_____
_____
_____
_____

Message to the Host:_____
_____
_____
_____
_____
_____

Welcome

Guest Name(s):_____ Date(s) of your stay:_____

Traveled From: _____

Favorite Beach House Memories:_____

_____
_____
_____
_____
_____
_____
_____

Recommendations (restaurants, entertainment, must-see sites):_____

_____
_____
_____
_____
_____
_____

Message to the Host:_____

_____
_____
_____
_____
_____

Welcome

Guest Name(s):_____ Date(s) of your stay:_____

Traveled From: _____

Favorite Beach House Memories: _____
_____
_____
_____
_____
_____
_____

Recommendations (restaurants, entertainment, must-see sites): _____
_____
_____
_____
_____
_____

Message to the Host:_____
_____
_____
_____
_____

Welcome

Guest Name(s):_____ Date(s) of your stay:_____

Traveled From: _____

Favorite Beach House Memories:_____

_____

_____

_____

_____

_____

_____

_____

Recommendations (restaurants, entertainment, must-see sites):_____

_____

_____

_____

_____

_____

_____

_____

Message to the Host:_____

_____

_____

_____

_____

_____

Welcome

Guest Name(s):_____ Date(s) of your stay:_____

Traveled From: _____

Favorite Beach House Memories:_____

_____
_____
_____
_____
_____
_____
_____

Recommendations (restaurants, entertainment, must-see sites):_____

_____
_____
_____
_____
_____
_____
_____

Message to the Host:_____

_____
_____
_____
_____
_____

Welcome

Guest Name(s):_____ Date(s) of your stay:_____

Traveled From: _____

Favorite Beach House Memories:_____

_____

_____

_____

_____

_____

_____

_____

Recommendations (restaurants, entertainment, must-see sites):_____

_____

_____

_____

_____

_____

_____

_____

Message to the Host:_____

_____

_____

_____

_____

_____

Welcome

Guest Name(s):_____ Date(s) of your stay:_____

Traveled From: _____

Favorite Beach House Memories:_____

_____
_____
_____
_____
_____
_____
_____

Recommendations (restaurants, entertainment, must-see sites):_____

_____
_____
_____
_____
_____
_____
_____

Message to the Host:_____

_____
_____
_____
_____
_____

Welcome

Guest Name(s):_____ Date(s) of your stay:_____

Traveled From: _____

Favorite Beach House Memories: _____

_____

_____

_____

_____

_____

_____

_____

Recommendations (restaurants, entertainment, must-see sites):_____

_____

_____

_____

_____

_____

_____

_____

Message to the Host:_____

_____

_____

_____

_____

_____

Welcome

Guest Name(s):_____ Date(s) of your stay:_____

Traveled From: _____

Favorite Beach House Memories:_____

_____

_____

_____

_____

_____

_____

Recommendations (restaurants, entertainment, must-see sites):_____

_____

_____

_____

_____

_____

_____

Message to the Host:_____

_____

_____

_____

_____

Welcome

Guest Name(s):_____ Date(s) of your stay:_____

Traveled From: _____

Favorite Beach House Memories:_____

_____
_____
_____
_____
_____
_____
_____

Recommendations (restaurants, entertainment, must-see sites):_____

_____
_____
_____
_____
_____
_____

Message to the Host:_____

_____
_____
_____
_____
_____

Welcome

Guest Name(s):_____ Date(s) of your stay:_____

Traveled From: _____

Favorite Beach House Memories:_____
_____
_____
_____
_____
_____
_____
_____

Recommendations (restaurants, entertainment, must-see sites):_____
_____
_____
_____
_____
_____
_____
_____

Message to the Host:_____
_____
_____
_____
_____
_____

Welcome

Guest Name(s):_____ Date(s) of your stay:_____

Traveled From: _____

Favorite Beach House Memories: _____

_____
_____
_____
_____
_____
_____
_____

Recommendations (restaurants, entertainment, must-see sites):_____

_____
_____
_____
_____
_____
_____
_____
_____

Message to the Host:_____

_____
_____
_____
_____
_____

Welcome

Guest Name(s):_____ Date(s) of your stay:_____

Traveled From: _____

Favorite Beach House Memories:_____

_____
_____
_____
_____
_____
_____

Recommendations (restaurants, entertainment, must-see sites):_____

_____
_____
_____
_____
_____
_____

Message to the Host:_____

_____
_____
_____
_____

Welcome

Guest Name(s):_____ Date(s) of your stay:_____

Traveled From: _____

Favorite Beach House Memories:_____
_____
_____
_____
_____
_____
_____
_____

Recommendations (restaurants, entertainment, must-see sites):_____
_____
_____
_____
_____
_____
_____

Message to the Host:_____
_____
_____
_____
_____
_____
_____

Welcome

Guest Name(s):_____ Date(s) of your stay:_____

Traveled From: _____

Favorite Beach House Memories:_____

_____
_____
_____
_____
_____
_____
_____

Recommendations (restaurants, entertainment, must-see sites):_____

_____
_____
_____
_____
_____
_____

Message to the Host:_____

_____
_____
_____
_____

Welcome

Guest Name(s):_____ Date(s) of your stay:_____

Traveled From: _____

Favorite Beach House Memories:_____
_____
_____
_____
_____
_____
_____
_____

Recommendations (restaurants, entertainment, must-see sites):_____
_____
_____
_____
_____
_____
_____

Message to the Host:_____
_____
_____
_____
_____
_____

Welcome

Guest Name(s):_____ Date(s) of your stay:_____

Traveled From: _____

Favorite Beach House Memories:_____
_____
_____
_____
_____
_____
_____
_____

Recommendations (restaurants, entertainment, must-see sites):_____
_____
_____
_____
_____
_____
_____

Message to the Host:_____
_____
_____
_____
_____
_____

Welcome

Guest Name(s):_____ Date(s) of your stay:_____

Traveled From: _____

Favorite Beach House Memories: _____
_____
_____
_____
_____
_____
_____
_____

Recommendations (restaurants, entertainment, must-see sites): _____
_____
_____
_____
_____
_____
_____

Message to the Host:_____
_____
_____
_____
_____
_____

Welcome

Guest Name(s):_____ Date(s) of your stay:_____

Traveled From: _____

Favorite Beach House Memories:_____

_____

_____

_____

_____

_____

_____

Recommendations (restaurants, entertainment, must-see sites):_____

_____

_____

_____

_____

_____

_____

_____

Message to the Host:_____

_____

_____

_____

_____

_____

Welcome

Guest Name(s):_____ Date(s) of your stay:_____

Traveled From: _____

Favorite Beach House Memories: _____
_____
_____
_____
_____
_____
_____
_____

Recommendations (restaurants, entertainment, must-see sites):_____
_____
_____
_____
_____
_____
_____
_____

Message to the Host:_____
_____
_____
_____
_____
_____

Welcome

Guest Name(s):_____ Date(s) of your stay:_____

Traveled From: _____

Favorite Beach House Memories: _____

_____
_____
_____
_____
_____
_____
_____

Recommendations (restaurants, entertainment, must-see sites):_____

_____
_____
_____
_____
_____
_____

Message to the Host:_____

_____
_____
_____
_____
_____

Welcome

Guest Name(s):_____ Date(s) of your stay:_____

Traveled From: _____

Favorite Beach House Memories: _____

_____

_____

_____

_____

_____

_____

_____

Recommendations (restaurants, entertainment, must-see sites): _____

_____

_____

_____

_____

_____

_____

Message to the Host:_____

_____

_____

_____

_____

Welcome

Guest Name(s):_____ Date(s) of your stay:_____

Traveled From: _____

Favorite Beach House Memories: _____

_____

_____

_____

_____

_____

_____

_____

Recommendations (restaurants, entertainment, must-see sites): _____

_____

_____

_____

_____

_____

_____

_____

Message to the Host:_____

_____

_____

_____

_____

Welcome

Guest Name(s):_____ Date(s) of your stay:_____

Traveled From: _____

Favorite Beach House Memories: _____
_____
_____
_____
_____
_____
_____
_____

Recommendations (restaurants, entertainment, must-see sites): _____
_____
_____
_____
_____
_____
_____

Message to the Host: _____
_____
_____
_____
_____
_____

Welcome

Guest Name(s):_____ Date(s) of your stay:_____

Traveled From: _____

Favorite Beach House Memories: _____
_____
_____
_____
_____
_____
_____

Recommendations (restaurants, entertainment, must-see sites): _____
_____
_____
_____
_____
_____
_____

Message to the Host:_____
_____
_____
_____
_____
_____

Welcome

Guest Name(s):_____ Date(s) of your stay:_____

Traveled From: _____

Favorite Beach House Memories: _____
_____
_____
_____
_____
_____
_____

Recommendations (restaurants, entertainment, must-see sites):_____
_____
_____
_____
_____
_____
_____

Message to the Host:_____
_____
_____
_____
_____

Welcome

Guest Name(s):_____ Date(s) of your stay:_____

Traveled From: _____

Favorite Beach House Memories: _____
_____
_____
_____
_____
_____
_____
_____

Recommendations (restaurants, entertainment, must-see sites): _____
_____
_____
_____
_____
_____
_____
_____

Message to the Host:_____
_____
_____
_____
_____
_____

Welcome

Guest Name(s):_____ Date(s) of your stay:_____

Traveled From: _____

Favorite Beach House Memories: _____

_____
_____
_____
_____
_____
_____
_____

Recommendations (restaurants, entertainment, must-see sites): _____

_____
_____
_____
_____
_____
_____

Message to the Host:_____

_____
_____
_____
_____
_____

Welcome

Guest Name(s):_____ Date(s) of your stay:_____

Traveled From: _____

Favorite Beach House Memories: _____

_____

_____

_____

_____

_____

_____

_____

Recommendations (restaurants, entertainment, must-see sites):_____

_____

_____

_____

_____

_____

_____

_____

_____

Message to the Host:_____

_____

_____

_____

_____

Welcome

Guest Name(s):_____ Date(s) of your stay:_____

Traveled From: _____

Favorite Beach House Memories: _____

_____
_____
_____
_____
_____
_____
_____
_____

Recommendations (restaurants, entertainment, must-see sites):_____

_____
_____
_____
_____
_____
_____
_____

Message to the Host:_____

_____
_____
_____
_____
_____

Thank you for purchasing this guest book!
We hope you love it! Please take a look at
some of our other products:
viewauthor.at/APPressly

Follow us on Social Media

 @A2PPress

 @a2p_press

Made in United States
Orlando, FL
16 July 2025

62988517R00059